DATE DUE

D1473076

1,001 Proverbs for Every Occasion

1,001 Proverbs for Every Occasion

Wise Thoughts and Insightful Advice
From Around the World

**COMPILED AND EDITED BY
NORMA GLEASON**

CITADEL PRESS
Kensington Publishing Corp.
www.kensingtonbooks.com

CITADEL PRESS books are published by

Kensington Publishing Corp.
850 Third Avenue
New York, NY 10022

Previously published as *A Fool in a Hurry Drinks Tea With a Fork*

All Kensington titles, imprints, and distributed lines are available at special quantity discounts for bulk purchases for sales promotions, premiums, fund raising, educational, or institutional use. Special book excerpts or customized printings can also be created to fit specific needs. For details, write or phone the office of the Kensington special sales manager: Kensington Publishing Corp., 850 Third Avenue, New York, NY 10022, attn: Special Sales Department, phone 1-800-221-2647.

Citadel Press and the Citadel logo are trademarks of Kensington Publishing Corp.

First printing April 2001

10 9 8 7 6 5 4 3 2 1

Printed in the United States of America

Library of Congress Cataloging-in-Publication Data

1001 proverbs for every occasion : wise thoughts and insightful advice
    from around the world / compiled and edited by Norma Gleason.
        p.   cm.
    Rev. ed. of: A fool in a hurry drinks tea with a fork. 1994
    ISBN 0-8065-2117-1 (hc)
    1. Proverbs.   I. Gleason, Norma.   II. Fool in a hurry drinks tea with a
fork.   III. Title: One thousand one proverbs for every occasion.   IV. Title:
One thousand and one proverbs for every occasion.
IN PROCESS PN6405.0
398.9—dc21   99–16392
                                                                          CIP

Contents

Acknowledgments

I OWE SPECIAL THANKS to Gene DeGruson, Special Collections Librarian of the E. Haldeman-Julius collection at the Leonard H. Axe library at Pittsburg (Kansas) State University. Mr. DeGruson kindly provided me with photocopies of the little proverb books from his collection, first published forty and fifty years ago.

I am also indebted to Dr. Leo Hamlian of Ararat Press, Saddle Brook, New Jersey, for permission to use Armenian proverbs from their book "Seven Bites from a Raisin"; and to Dr. Kermit Westbrook of Augustana College, Rock Island, Illinois for providing me with hard-to-find Swedish proverbs from their private collection.

Last but not least I need to thank John and Elaine Gill of The Crossing Press for permission to use proverbs from "The Proverb Book."

I have also taken the liberty of judiciously borrowing a few proverbs here and there from other large published volumes and express gratitude for these borrowings. They constitute a minor portion of the proverbs in this book.

Norma Gleason

*1,001 Proverbs for
Every Occasion*

Introduction

COLLECTING PROVERBS FOR THIS BOOK was both fun and educational. I discovered that through proverbs, every language reveals the unique attitudes and culture of its people. French proverbs, I found, tend to be philosophical and intellectual, as with "If the triangles had a god, they would give him three sides." Irish and Scottish proverbs embody a caustic wit: "Ye come from the McTakes, but not from the McGives" (Scottish). And Russian proverbs show a stoic acceptance of whatever fate deals out: "If there is no apple, one eats a little carrot."

Although, as a rule, the line between quotations and proverbs is distinct, it is not so easy to distinguish among old sayings, proverbs and certain quotations that have passed into the sphere of proverb lore, such as Benjamin Franklin's "A word to the wise is sufficient." A few proverbs in this book may be classified by some scholars as proverbs and by other scholars as old sayings.

Proverbs travel from country to country. The Spanish say "En tierra de ciegos, el tuerto es rey." The French express the same thought in their own language, as we do when we say in English, "In the land of the blind, the one-eyed is king."

Or the same thought is expressed in totally different words, reflecting differing lifestyles. English-speaking peoples say "Give him an inch and he'll take a mile." The Arab version of this philosophy is "Let the camel get his nose in the tent and the body will soon follow."

Proverbs often deal with man's disillusionment with his lot. An Arab may wail, "If I sold winding sheets, no one would die," and a Spaniard complain, "I wept when I was born, and every day explains why."

For the convenience of writers and speakers, the proverbs are sorted out into categories from *Advice* to *Wishful Thinking*. Under each category heading the proverbs are listed alphabetically by origin.

May you enjoy browsing among these proverbs as much as I have enjoyed collecting them.

ADVICE

1. Advice given in the midst of a crowd is loathsome.
   Arab

2. When the cart breaks down, advice is plentiful.
   Armenian

3. Nobody will give a pauper bread, but everybody
   will give him advice.   *Armenian*

4. If I had given fourpence for the advice, I bought it a
   groat too dear.   *English*

5. We should never be ashamed to take advice, even
   from the lowly.   *German*

6. Do not give advice unless you have the wisdom to
   go with it.   *Irish*

7. Teeth placed before the tongue give good advice.
   Italian

8. Himself in disgrace, he gives other free advice.
   Persian

9. I gave so much advice that hair grew on my tongue.
   Persian

10. The wise must be respected, even when the advice
    they give us is not suitable.   *Sanskrit*

11. A woman's advice is of little value, but he who does
    not take it is a fool.   *Spanish*

AGE

12. To succeed, consult three old people.   *Chinese*

13. Every age wants its playthings.   *French*

14. When we are old, all our pleasures are behind us,
    but when we are young, all our troubles are before
    us.   *Irish*

15. When a lion is old, he becomes the plaything of
    jackals.   *Persian*

16. At twenty a man will be a peacock, at thirty a lion,
    at forty a camel, at fifty a serpent, at sixty a dog, at
    seventy a monkey and at eighty nothing.   *Spanish*

17. The young should be taught, the old should be honored. *Swedish*

18. A man shows in his youth what he will be in his age. *Yugoslav*

ATTITUDES

19. Do not ridicule the thin-bearded when you yourself have no beard. *Arab*

20. Can one start a fast with baklava in one's hand? *Armenian*

21. A man who cannot tolerate small ills can never accomplish great things. *Chinese*

22. The thief is sorry that he is to be hanged, not that he is a thief. *English*

23. People who live in glass houses shouldn't throw stones. *English*

24. In the land of the blind, the one-eyed is king. *French*

25. The most wasted of all days is the day when we have not laughed. *French*

26. A man is no happier than he thinks himself. *French*

27. If you cannot catch a fish, do not blame the sea. *Greek*
28. The fox that had her tail cut off tried to entice the others to imitate her. *Greek*
29. If you call a lady a slave, she laughs, but if you call a slave a slave, she cries. *Hindustan*
30. He that has a jaundiced eye sees everything yellow. *India*
31. Is it necessary to add acid to the lemon? *India*
32. The pot broken by the mother-in-law was a cracked pot; the pot broken by the daughter-in-law was a new pot. *India*
33. All the turf in the bog wouldn't warm me to him. *Irish*
34. The heaviest ear of corn is the one with its head bent low. *Irish*
35. The would-be buyer always depreciates. *Italian*
36. A man with a sour face should not open a shop. *Japanese*
37. Cold rice and cold tea are bearable, but cold looks and cold words are not. *Japanese*
38. By one ear he hears, and by the other he dismisses. *Persian*

39. The shovel insults the poker.   *Russian*
40. It will last out our time; if after us no grass grows, what does it matter to us?   *Russian*
41. To ask is no sin, and to be refused is no calamity.   *Russian*
42. If a man's heart be impure, all things will appear hostile to him.   *Sanskrit*
43. It is not the fault of the post that a blind man cannot see it.   *Sanskrit*
44. They know not their own defects who search for the defects of others.   *Sanskrit*
45. The tree that is cut down grows again; the moon that wanes after a time waxes again. Thus do wise men reflect and, though distressed, are not overwhelmed.   *Sanskrit*
46. He that has a big nose thinks everyone speaks of it.   *Scottish*
47. If I die, I forgive you; if I recover, we shall see.   *Spanish*
48. The good man cannot always escape calumny.   *Spanish*
49. What matter if I suffer, if only my neighbor suffers too.   *Swedish*

50. We should think and speak well of each other.
    Swedish
51. If you would call the dog to you, do not carry a
    stick.   *West Africa*
52. The sparrow says, "I did not eat, therefore the
    parrot should not eat."   *West Africa*
53. There is no medicine to cure hatred.   *West Africa*
54. A bowl should not laugh when a calabash breaks.
    West Africa
55. When one is not good oneself, one likes to talk of
    what is wrong with others.   *Yugoslav*
56. It is better to look from the mountain than from the
    dungeon.   *Yugoslav*

AUTHORITY

57. Authority brooks no partner.   *French*
58. The strong obey when the stronger order.   *Irish*
59. The horse may wish to do one thing, but he who
    saddles him another.   *Spanish*
60. Who gives the bread lays down the authority.
    Spanish
61. Permission is needless to him who has the power to
    take without it.   *Spanish*

62. It is pleasant to command, be it only a herd of cattle.   *Spanish*

63. Where the water rules, the land submits.
    West Africa

64. When the big bells ring, the little bells are not heard.   *Yugoslav*

65. He who does not know how to serve cannot know how to command.   *Yugoslav*

66. If you wish to know what a man is, place him in authority.   *Yugoslav*

BEAUTY

67. Beauty is power.   *Arab*
68. Though the peony be beautiful, it must be supported by green leaves.   *Chinese*
69. Beauty is only skin deep.   *English*
70. Beauty is the eye's food but the soul's sorrow.   *German*
71. What does the blind man know of the beauty of the tulip?   *Hindustan*
72. Beauty does not make the pot boil.   *Irish*
73. Beauty is only skin deep, but nobody wants to be drowned.   *Irish*
74. What worth has beauty if it not be seen?   *Italian*

75. Is there anything naturally beautiful or not beautiful? Whatever is pleasing to anyone, that is beautiful for him.   *Sanskrit*
76. The voice is the beauty of cuckoos; chastity is the beauty of women; learning is the beauty of the deformed; patience is the beauty of ascetics. *Sanskrit*
77. Lovely flowers fade fast. Weeds last the season. *Swedish*
78. A chicken with beautiful plumage does not sit in a corner.   *West Africa*

BEGGARS

79. If begging should unfortunately be your lot, knock at the large gates only.   *Arab*
80. Beggars can't be choosers.   *English*
81. A beggar on his feet is worth more than an emperor in his grave.   *French*
82. Though you are going begging, go decently attired.   *India*
83. If a beggar be placed in the midst of a grove of pear trees, even there he will beg.   *India*
84. Constant begging means constant refusal.   *Irish*

85. A beggar won't mind being insulted.   *West Africa*
86. The best morsels are never given to a beggar.
West Africa

Behavior

87. When the market is brisk, the seller does not stop to wash the mud from his turnips.   *Chinese*
88. If you bow at all, bow low.   *Chinese*
89. Some have been thought brave because they were afraid to run away.   *English*
90. Charity begins at home.   *English*
91. Ye be as full of good manners as an egg be of oatmeal.   *English*
92. From a short pleasure comes a long repentance. *French*
93. Let everyone carry his own sack to the mill. *German*
94. It is little honor to the lion to seize the mouse. *German*
95. When you go to bed with a clear head, you will never rise with a headache.   *Greek*
96. If you are a priest, be a priest; if you are a plowman, be a plowman.   *Greek*

97. Dependence on another is perpetual disappointment.
    Hindustan

98. Who will pay for the shoe of a partnership horse?
    India

99. It is easy to forget a kindness, but one remembers
    unkindness. *India*

100. It is not for the blind to give an opinion on colors.
     Italian

101. Do not prophesy to the man who can see further
     than you can. *Japanese*

102. He cries before he is beaten. *Persian*

103. Be bad to the bad and good to the good; be a
     flower unto a flower and a thorn unto a
     thorn. *Persian*

104. Make thyself a sheep and the wolf is ready.
     Russian

105. If men could foresee the future, they would still
     behave as they do now. *Russian*

106. Do not spit into the well—you may have to drink
     out of it. *Russian*

107. An ill-tempered question deserves an ill-tempered
     answer. *Scottish*

108. Lock your door and preserve your neighbor's honor. *Spanish*

109. She alone is chaste who has never been sought. *Spanish*

110. Kindness begets kindness. *Swedish*

111. Fear less, hope more. Eat less, chew more. Sigh less, breathe more. Hate less, love more, and all good things are yours. *Swedish*

112. When you are among the blind, shut your eyes. *Turkish*

113. At meal time, "Yes!" When duty calls, "No!" *West Africa*

114. Condemn a man within his hearing; praise him when he is away. *Yugoslav*

115. He who humbles himself too much gets trampled upon. *Yugoslav*

BELIEF

116. There are no mistakes to the man who does not believe in them. *French*

117. To believe everything is too much, to believe nothing is not enough. *German*

118. Don't believe everything you hear nor tell all that you know. *Italian*
119. The more one knows, the less one believes. *Italian*
120. Believe all ye hear and ye may eat all ye see. *Scottish*
121. Of what you see, believe very little, of what you are told, nothing. *Spanish*

BOOKS

122. You cannot open a book without learning something. *Chinese*
123. God deliver me from a man of one book. *English*
124. Every abridgement of a good book is a stupid abridgement. *French*
125. A book, to a blind man, signifies nothing. *Irish*
126. He who lends a book, one of his hands should be cut off. He who returns it, both his hands should be cut off. *Persian*

CAUTION

127. The dry reed does not seek the company of the fire. *Arab*
128. The chameleon does not leave one tree until he is sure of another. *Arab*
129. The mouse that has but one hole is soon caught. *Arab*
130. Don't pour away the water you are traveling with because of a mirage. *Arab*
131. While the cautious one ponders, the fool will cross the bridge. *Armenian*
132. He who was bitten by a snake avoids tall grass. *Chinese*

133. Before you beat the dog, learn the name of his master. *Chinese*
134. Look before you leap. *English*
135. Forewarned is forearmed. *English*
136. Don't buy a pig in a poke. *English*
137. He who has burned his tongue does not forget to blow on the soup. *German*
138. A flatterer has water in one hand and fire in the other. *German*
139. Do not lean on a worm-eaten staff. *Greek*
140. He who has been scalded with hot milk blows even on buttermilk before he drinks it. *Hindustan*
141. Though the snake be small, it is wise to hit it with a big stick. *India*
142. Never put your hand out further than you can draw it back again. *Irish*
143. The best armor is to keep out of gunshot. *Italian*
144. By poking at a bamboo thicket, you may drive out a snake. *Japanese*
145. Trust in God, but tie your camel. *Persian*
146. If a man knew where he would fall, he would spread a carpet first. *Russian*

147. Look before ye leap and ye'll ken better to light.
Scottish

148. The blind man's peck should be well measured.
Scottish

149. If ye cannot see the bottom, do not wade far out.
Scottish

150. It's good to be civil, as the old wife said when she beckoned to the devil.   *Scottish*

151. When the cup is full, carry it even.   *Scottish*

152. The scalded cat flees even from cold water.
Spanish

153. In large rivers one finds big fish but one may also be drowned.   *Spanish*

154. Don't wake up sleeping sadness.   *Swedish*

155. Measure forty times, cut once.   *Turkish*

156. The lamb that strays from the field will be eaten by the wolf.   *Turkish*

157. He who has been bitten by a snake avoids the tall grass.   *Yugoslav*

158. No one likes to be the first to step on ice.
Yugoslav

CHARACTER

159. If your beard were on fire, he'd light his cigarette on it.   *Armenian*

160. It is better to do a kindness near home than go far to burn incense.   *Chinese*

161. Still waters run deep.   *English*

162. It is a double pleasure to deceive the deceiver.   *French*

163. Talent is born in silence but character is born in the struggle of life.   *German*

164. He who holds the ladder is as bad as the thief.   *German*

165. He who goes unpunished never learns.   *Greek*

166. A snake will emit only poison even though you feed it on milk.   *India*

167. He would cover a rock with hay and sell it for a haystack.   *Irish*

168. A fair character is a fair fortune.   *Irish*

169. He'd give you an egg if you promised not to break the shell.   *Irish*

170. You can't judge a man's respectability by the size of his prayer book.   *Irish*

171. He is so stingy that if he gave you the measles, it would be one measle at a time.   *Irish*
172. Titles do not make men illustrious; men make their titles illustrious.   *Italian*
173. Of two cowards, the one who finds the other out first has the advantage.   *Italian*
174. Even if you put a snake in a bamboo tube, you cannot change its wriggling disposition.   *Japanese*
175. Look the other way when a girl at the teahouse smiles.   *Japanese*
176. A good reputation sits still, a bad one runs about.   *Russian*
177. Fortune attends the man who exerts himself. They are weak who declare fate the sole cause.   *Sanskrit*
178. Inactivity from fear of committing a fault is the mark of a coward. By whom is food renounced for fear of indigestion?   *Sanskrit*
179. Ye come from the McTakes but not from the McGives.   *Scottish*
180. They are free with their horse who have none.   *Scottish*
181. Honor is the throne of integrity.   *Spanish*

182. If guilt were a robe of sable nobody would wear it.   *Turkish*

183. Where there is no shame, there is no honor.
West Africa

184. If you refuse to be made straight when you are green, you will not be made straight when you are dry.   *West Africa*

185. He is not honest who has burned his tongue and does not tell the company the soup is hot.   *Yugoslav*

CHILDREN

186. To understand your parent's love, bear your own children.   *Chinese*

187. A growing youth has a wolf in his stomach.
English

188. Children should be seen and not heard.   *English*

189. Spare the rod and spoil the child.   *English*

190. Little pitchers have big ears.   *English*

191. One father can support twelve children, but twelve children cannot support one father.   *French*

192. In the young, silence is better than speech.   *Greek*

193. Rear and nourish children with kindness, but chastise with severity.   *Hindustan*

194. The baby is not yet born, and yet you say that his nose is like his grandfather's.   *India*

195. Bricks and mortar make a house but the laughter of children make a home.   *Irish*

196. When children are little they make our heads ache; when grown, our hearts.   *Italian*

197. Children are the poor man's treasure.   *Japanese*

198. Excessive praise spoils the child.   *Persian*

199. If the child does not cry the mother knows not it wants.   *Russian*

200. By wise people, an appropriate observation is accepted even from a child. On the invisibility of the sun, is not the light of a lamp availed of?   *Sanskrit*

201. They were scant o' bairns that brought you up.   *Scottish*

202. Bairns are certain care but no sure joy.   *Scottish*

203. Bachelor's wives and old maids' bairns are always well bred.   *Scottish*

204. Ye'll learn your father to get bairns.   *Scottish*

205. The bairn speaks in the fields what he heard by the hearth.   *Scottish*
206. A child's love is water in a basket.   *Spanish*
207. Children act in the village as they have learned at home.   *Swedish*
208. He who has no children has one sorrow, he who has children has a thousand sorrows.   *Turkish*
209. If you have good children, why do you need wealth? And if you have bad children, again why do you need wealth?   *Turkish*
210. You complain about your neighbor's children. How about your own?   *West Africa*
211. Woe to the man who relies upon his children's help.   *Yugoslav*

COMMON SENSE

212. Do not dress in leaf-made clothes when going to put out a fire.   *Chinese*
213. The fox invited the chicken to dinner; the chicken politely declined.   *Greek*
214. If you put it in the tank do not seek it in the well.   *India*

215. If common sense rules from your head to your feet, you'll not wear a dunce cap or walk a wrong road.   *Irish*
216. Before you buy shoes, measure your feet.   *West Africa*

COMPANIONS

217. Live with him who prays and you will pray, live with him who sings and you will sing.   *Arab*
218. The crow does not roost with the phoenix.   *Chinese*
219. Touch black paint and you will have black fingers.   *Chinese*
220. Birds of a feather flock together.   *English*
221. If you have no arrows in your quiver, do not go with archers.   *German*
222. A dove has no place amongst the crows.   *Greek*
223. Whatever is in the pot will come onto the ladle.   *Hindustan*
224. In the friendship of an ass expect nothing but kicks.   *India*
225. Know a horse by riding him; a person by associating with him.   *Japanese*

226. A thief knows a thief and a saint a saint.   *Persian*
227. Keep good company and ye will be counted one of them.   *Scottish*
228. Eagles fly alone but sheep flock together.   *Scottish*
229. Leopards and goats do not associate with each other in herds.   *West Africa*
230. If it is difficult to know a man, find out with whom he associates. You will then know him. *Yugoslav*

COMPETENCE

231. A good archer is known not by his arrows but by his aim.   *English*
232. The good seaman can be recognized when the storm comes.   *Greek*
233. The load of an elephant can be carried only by the elephant.   *Hindustan*
234. Under a powerful general there are no feeble soldiers.   *Japanese*
235. To a good rider, right or left makes no difference. *Turkish*

CONFIDENCE

236. Confidence brings more to conversation than does wit.   *French*
237. The man who has mounted an elephant will not fear the bark of a dog.   *India*
238. The biggest of serpents has no terrors for the eagle.   *Japanese*
239. What fear has he whose account is clean?   *Persian*

CONSCIENCE

240. The man whose conscience is easy will never fear a knock on the door at midnight.   *Chinese*
241. Better a good conscience without wisdom than wisdom without a good conscience.   *German*
242. Conscience chastises the soul.   *Greek*
243. May we always have a clean shirt, a clean conscience and a bob in the pocket.   *Irish*
244. A good conscience is God's eye.   *Russian*
245. A safe conscience makes a sound sleep.   *Scottish*

CONSEQUENCES

246. If you strike mud against the wall, even though it does not stick, it will leave a mark. *Arab*

247. He shall reap hemp who sows hemp, and beans who sows beans. *Chinese*

248. He that blows in the fire must expect sparks in his eyes. *German*

249. From a wormy walnut tree you will gather wormy walnuts. *Greek*

250. If you sleep with a dog you will rise full of fleas. *Greek*

251. The butterfly that sports around the lamplight will surely burn her wings. *Greek*

252. If you plant a mango then you may eat a mango. *Hindustan*

253. He that digs a pit for another may fall into it himself. *Hindustan*

254. I sowed seeds of acacia; whence shall I eat raisins? *Hindustan*

255. One must accept the cow's kick as well as her milk and butter. *India*

256. The more you step on the dunghill, the more dirt you'll get into. *Irish*

257. He who is an ass and takes himself to be a stag finds his mistake when he comes to leap the ditch.   *Italian*

258. Flies will never leave the shop of a sweetmaker. *Persian*

259. Where you saw wood, there the sawdust will fall.   *Russian*

260. He must stoop who has a low door.   *Scottish*

261. He who peeps through a hole may see what will vex him.   *Spanish*

262. "If" and "when" were planted, and "nothing" grew.   *Turkish*

263. It rained on the mountaintop, but it was the valley below that got flooded.   *West Africa*

CONTENTMENT

264. Go along with old shoes until God brings you new shoes.   *Arab*

265. I have plenty of apples and pears, but my heart yearns for quince.   *Armenian*

266. Be contented with whatever you have.   *Chinese*

267. No news is good news.   *English*

268. A bird in the hand is worth two in the bush.
English

269. He who has everything is content with nothing.
French

270. Contentment is worth more than riches.   *German*

271. The mosque has fallen, but the pulpit
stands.   *Hindustan*

272. When the bed breaks, there is the ground to lie
on.   *India*

273. A harvest of peace is produced from a seed of
contentment.   *India*

274. Stretch your limbs according to your sheet.   *India*

275. Firelight will not let you read fine stories, but it's
warm and you won't see the dust on the floor.
Irish

276. Be happy with what you have, and you will have
plenty to be happy about.   *Irish*

277. He who knows not when he has enough, is
poor.   *Japanese*

278. The sky is the same color wherever you go.
Persian

279. As long as the sun shines one does not ask for the
moon.   *Russian*

280. Desire upon desire cause the greatest sorrow; contentment, the greatest happiness. *Sanskrit*

281. Better a wee fire to warm you than a big fire to burn you. *Scottish*

282. On a day when you can dine on dry bread in your own house, do not seek to eat tender peacocks in the house of another. *Spanish*

283. That which one cannot have one should not desire. *Swedish*

284. A thing that is out of my reach is useless to me. *West Africa*

285. A cow must graze where it is tied. *West Africa*

286. What is impossible to change is best to forget. *Yugoslav*

COOPERATION

287. No matter how stout, one beam cannot support a house. *Chinese*

288. Two heads are better than one. *English*

289. If several join in an enterprise, then there is no disgrace should they fail. *Hindustan*

290. Three helping one another will do as much as six men singly. *Spanish*

291. In the forest, tree leans on tree, in a nation, man on man. *Yugoslav*

DEATH

292. When you are dead, your sister's tears will dry as time goes on, your widow's tears will cease in another's arms, but your mother will mourn you until she dies.   *Arab*

293. The first breath is the beginning of death.   *English*

294. One had as well be nibbled to death by ducks as pecked to death by hens.   *English*

295. Dead men tell no tales.   *English*

296. We should weep for men at their birth, not at their death.   *French*

297. Death is far better than the fear of death.   *French*

298. One has only to die to be praised.   *German*

299. Luck is for the few, death for the many.   *German*

300. You cannot go to heaven unless you yourself die. *India*

301. That which blossoms must also decay. *India*

302. Ink stains may be removed by washing, but natural dispositions disappear only in dying. *India*

303. May you never die until you see your own funeral. *Irish*

304. Better a coward than a corpse. *Irish*

305. There'll be many a dry eye at his death. *Irish*

306. Day by day death approaches, like the slaughter of a victim being led along step by step. *Sanskrit*

307. Wealth stops at the house, friends and relatives at the grave, but good deeds and evil deeds follow the dying man. *Sanskrit*

308. He that sits with his back to a draft, sits with his face to a coffin. *Spanish*

309. The dead are not seen in the company of the living. *West Africa*

DESPERATION

310. A drowning man takes hold of his own hair. *Greek*

311. Desperation is the mistress of the impossible.
Spanish

312. He who falls into the sea will cling even to a
snake. *Turkish*

313. Care avails nothing against fate. *Arab*

DESTINY

314. If a man's fate is to have only eight-tenths of a pint
of rice, though he traverse the country over, he
cannot get a full pint. *Chinese*

315. He that was born under a three half-penny planet
shall never be worth two pence. *English*

316. What must be, must be. *French*

317. Nothing can be erased from God's book. *Irish*

318. He that is born of a hen must scratch. *Italian*

319. When its time has arrived, the prey comes to the
hunter. *Persian*

320. He who is destined for the gallows will not be
drowned. *Russian*

321. An unguarded object remains safe if protected by
destiny; stricken by destiny, it perishes though well-
guarded. *Sanskrit*

322. After happiness, sorrow; after sorrow, happiness; happiness and sorrow revolve like a disc. *Sanskrit*

323. A many may woo where he may, but he must marry where his fate is. *Scottish*

324. When God ordains that one should die in the dark, it avails nothing that one's father is a wax chandler. *Spanish*

325. One can choose the clover yet end up in weeds. *Swedish*

326. Blood that is to flow will not stay in the veins. *Turkish*

327. Let no man think he can escape his fate. *West Africa*

DIFFERENCES

328. Variety is the spice of life. *English*

329. Whatever is natural possesses variety. *French*

330. Every tale can be told in a different way. *Greek*

331. A man with a nose is infamous among a hundred noseless men. *Hindustan*

332. There are as many characters as there are individuals. *India*

333. Ten men, ten minds. *Japanese*

334. If every day was a sunny day, who would not wish for rain? *Japanese*
335. John has one custom and Jack another. *Russian*
336. No two things are exactly alike. *West Africa*
337. Even the fingers on one's hand are not alike. *Yugoslav*

DRINK

338. The drunken man laughs without cause. *Arab*
339. Whoever drinks on credit gets drunk more quickly. *Armenian*
340. To stop drinking, study a drunkard when you are sober. *Chinese*
341. Drink wine and have the gout; drink none and have it anyway. *English*
342. He that killeth when he is drunk is hanged when he is sober. *English*
343. A drunkard who has taken the pledge should never be locked up in a wine cellar. *French*
344. When your wine flask is full, many friends can be made. *Greek*
345. If you drink even milk under a date tree, they will say it is toddy. *India*

346. Do not be talkative in an ale house.   *Irish*

347. He'd go to mass every morning if holy water were whiskey.   *Irish*

348. When you look at the world through the bottom of a glass, may you see someone ready to buy.   *Irish*

349. Take physic for healing, soup for nourishment and sake for happy living.   *Japanese*

350. Though the drunkard be in church, people will always suppose him to be in the public house.   *Russian*

351. More are drowned in drink than in water.   *Scottish*

352. He speaks in his drink what he thinks in his drouth.   *Scottish*

353. Wine has two defects: If you add water to it, you ruin it; if you do not add water, it ruins you.   *Spanish*

354. When the rich man falls down it is an accident; when a poor man falls, he is called a drunk.   *Turkish*

355. If you do not live near a wine palm you will not be tempted to drink palm wine.   *West Africa*

356. If I cannot propose a toast, at least I can drink the wine.   *Yugoslav*

357. Wine from a pot is better than water from a well.
Yugoslav

358. The drunkard reforms when he keels into his grave.
Yugoslav

ENVY

359. Compete, don't envy.   *Arab*
360. Envy accomplishes nothing.   *Greek*
361. It is not good for the eyes to smart in looking at another's goods.   *India*
362. Lepers are always envious of those with simple sores.   *Japanese*
363. In the hands of our neighbor, the morsel always appears big.   *Russian*
364. The fishes envy the carp on account of his shears.   *West Africa*
365. If envy would burn, there would be no use of wood.   *Yugoslav*

EQUALITY

366. He who rides the chair is a man like those who carry it.   *Chinese*
367. What's sauce for the goose is sauce for the gander.   *English*
368. The peasant reaches heaven as soon as the nobleman.   *German*
369. Those who live in houses are proud, but there is a God even for those who live in huts.   *India*
370. Six feet of earth makes us all of one size.   *Italian*
371. He who sits in, and he who pulls the rickshaw, are alike men.   *Japanese*
372. He who holds the stirrup is as good as he who mounts the horse.   *Scottish*

ERROR

373. Rather a slip of the foot than a slip of the pen.   *Arab*
374. What good is running if one is on the wrong road?   *English*
375. It is always necessary to start from a truth in order to teach an error.   *French*

376. A wise man will not err twice in the same way.
Greek

377. If you take the wrong hat from a meeting, make sure it doesn't belong to a big man.   *Irish*

378. From seeing smoke rising from one house, we do not infer that there is a fire in another house.
Sanskrit

379. He is always right who suspects that he is always making mistakes.   *Spanish*

380. Through mistakes one becomes wise.   *West Africa*

381. First to make a mistake, first to be laughed at.
West Africa

EXCUSES

382. They said to the camel bird (ostrich) "Carry!" It said, "I cannot, for I am a bird," They said "Then fly." It replied "I cannot, for I am a camel."   *Arab*

383. When they asked the fish "Have you news from the sea?" she answered, "I have much to say but my mouth is full of water."   *Armenian*

384. Ask a kite for a feather and she will say she has just enough to fly.   *English*

385. He who makes excuses accuses himself.   *French*

386. To make excuses before they are needed is to blame one's self.   *Spanish*

EXPERIENCE

387. The tongue of experience has the most truth.
     Arab
388. To know the road ahead, ask those coming back.
     Chinese
389. Experience is a hard school but a fool will learn in no other.   *Irish*
390. Sense bought by experience is better than two senses learned.   *Irish*
391. Pinch yourself and know how others feel.   *Japanese*
392. It is not the same to talk of bulls as to be in the bull ring.   *Spanish*

Faults and Virtues

393. The first half of the night, think of your own faults, the second half, the faults of others. *Chinese*
394. He never lies but when the holly's green. *English*
395. A fault denied is twice committed. *French*
396. The first and second faults may be forgiven, but the third stamps the miscreant. *Hindustan*
397. When faults are scrutinized, the relationships cease. *India*
398. Wink at small faults, for you have great ones yourself. *Scottish*
399. It is well that all our faults are not written in our face. *Scottish*

FINALITY

400. Four things cannot be brought back: a word spoken, an arrow discharged, the Divine decree, and past time. *Arab*

401. The swiftest horse cannot overtake the word once spoken. *Chinese*

402. All's well that end's well. *English*

403. He laughs best who laughs last. *English*

404. Everything passes, everything perishes, everything palls. *French*

405. It is too late to cover the well when the child is drowned. *German*

406. After conception, there is nothing for it but to bring forth. *India*

407. Once fallen, the blossom does not return to the branch. *Japanese*

408. The arrow which leaves the bow cannot come back. *Persian*

409. A word is not a bird; once flown you can never catch it. *Russian*

410. As the journey is ended by walking, so the debt is paid by paying. *Turkish*

411. No chicken will fall into the fire a second time.
West Africa

412. Hours once lost cannot be regained.　*Yugoslav*

FOOLS

413. A fool in a hurry drinks tea with a fork.
Chinese

414. A vacant mind is open to all suggestions, as a hollow building echoes all sounds.　*Chinese*

415. Expectation is the fool's income.　*English*

416. The young talk about what they are doing; the old about what they have done; fools about what they plan to do.　*French*

417. He is a fool who drives the cow of a stranger's out of a field which is also a stranger's.　*Hindustan*

418. A hundred wise men have the same opinion, but fools have every one their own.　*India*

419. When fools make mistakes, they lay the blame on Providence.　*Irish*

420. He who knows but little presently outs with it.
Italian

421. Learning without wisdom is a load of books on an ass's back.　*Japanese*

422. If they sent you even to the sea, you would not be able to find water.   *Persian*

423. The drum is boisterous to no avail; there is nothing in it.   *Persian*

424. By the time make a man of thee, I will myself have become a fool.   *Persian*

425. If all fools wore white caps we should look like a flock of sheep.   *Russian*

426. It is better to wander in a mountain pass with wild beasts than to live in the palace of the gods with a fool.   *Sanskrit*

427. God send ye more sense and me more silver.
Scottish

428. Wit without discretion is a sword in the hand of a fool.   *Spanish*

429. It is easier for a camel to jump over a pit than for the stupid to grasp what you say.   *Turkish*

430. By the time the fool has learned the game, the players have dispersed.   *West Africa*

FOOLISHNESS

431. Do not order the tree to be cut down which gives you shade.   *Arab*

432. He is looking for the donkey while sitting on it. *Armenian*

433. He can't even pull on his own britches, and he's running off to Baghdad. *Armenian*

434. Do not tear down the east wall to repair the west. *Chinese*

435. To sing to the deaf, to talk with the dumb, and to dance for the blind are three foolish things. *Hindustan*

436. The child is in his arms, yet he proclaims it lost in the city. *Hindustan*

437. It is foolish to hold a candle before the sun or turn a somersault before a monkey. *India*

438. Talking with a fool is like pouring water into an inverted pitcher. *India*

439. Never send a chicken to bring home a fox. *Irish*

440. He got up from the ground and sat on the ashes. *Persian*

441. He puts his cheese in a bottle and rubs his bread on the outside. *Persian*

442. Do not cover your neighbor's roof while your own is leaking. *Russian*

443. He had fine knowledge of horse flesh who bought a goose to ride on.   *Scottish*

444. The height of nonsense is suppin' sour milk with a fork.   *Scottish*

445. If folly were grief, there would be weeping in every house.   *Spanish*

446. Don't cross the stream to find water.   *Swedish*

447. He paid more for the lining than for the cloth.   *Turkish*

448. A foolish act done over again will not improve things.   *West Africa*

FRIENDS AND ENEMIES

449. Let us quarrel with our friend rather than be too long friendly with our enemy.   *Arab*

450. Predestined enemies will always meet in a narrow alleyway.   *Chinese*

451. If you have money and wine, your friends will be many.   *Chinese*

452. A friend in need is a friend indeed.   *English*

453. A hedge between keeps friendship green.   *English*

454. It is more shameful to distrust one's friends than to be deceived by them.   *French*

455. When there is no enemy it is safe fighting.
German

456. Friendship is a plant we must often water.   *German*

457. Everyone's companion is no one's friend.   *German*

458. To lose a friend, make him a loan.   *Greek*

459. A good man finds all the world friendly.
Hindustan

460. Though your enemy be a hundred miles off, act as if he were visible beside your bed.   *India*

461. Prove a friend before you seek him.   *Irish*

462. Men of the same trade are enemies.   *Persian*

463. Make friendship with the wolf, but keep your axe ready.   *Russian*

464. A thousand friends are few; one enemy is too many.   *Russian*

465. He is wise that can make a friend of a foe.   *Scottish*

466. If thy enemy is an ant, regard him as an elephant.   *Turkish*

467. Boast to a stranger, complain only to your friends.
Yugoslav

FUTILE EXPECTATIONS

468. You cannot fill your belly by painting pictures of bread. *Chinese*

469. Though the ant works its heart out, it can never make honey. *English*

470. The frog wanted to be an ox and swelled up until he burst. *Greek*

471. From a broken violin do not expect fine music. *Greek*

472. The crane, hoping to eat dried fish when the sea dried up, wasted away in expectancy. *India*

473. It's no use going to the goat's house to look for wool. *Irish*

474. One cannot lap up the ocean with a shell. *Japanese*

475. He who remains hopeful of his neighbor's help will have to go to bed dinnerless. *Persian*

476. One cannot learn to swim in a field. *Spanish*

477. The frog saw the horse being shod and presented his feet also. *Turkish*

478. From lean meat do not expect fat broth. *Turkish*

479. A fire will not be quenched by adding more fuel.   *West Africa*

480. One cannot possibly bake bread for the entire world.   *Yugoslav*

Good and Evil

481. Evil people know one another. *Arab*

482. A man cannot become perfect in a hundred years; but he may become corrupt in less than one day. *Chinese*

483. Every evil comes to us on wings and goes away limping. *French*

484. When one evil comes, a million follow it. *Greek*

485. Every man is the guardian of his own honor. *Hindustan*

486. It's often the most wicked who know the nearest path to the shrine. *Japanese*

487. A thread will tie an honest man better than a rope will tie a knave. *Scottish*

488. Evil knows the sleeping place of evil.   *West Africa*

489. It is not easy to meet good, but it is easy to recognize it.   *Yugoslav*

GREED

490. Greed lessens what is gathered.   *Arab*

491. Give him an inch and he'll take a mile.   *English*

492. He has a larger eye than a stomach.   *Greek*

493. If he is allowed to touch your finger, he will speedily seize your wrist.   *Hindustan*

494. The greedy man stores all but friendship.   *Irish*

495. Avarice closes the eyes of even a sensible man. Is it not greed that brings birds and fishes into nets? *Persian*

496. He is in the water up to the neck and is clamoring for a drink.   *Russian*

497. Greedy folk have long arms.   *Scottish*

498. One who grabs too much may lose it all.   *Swedish*

499. Who asks at once for much returns home with an empty bag.   *Yugoslav*

GUESTS

500. The guest of the hospitable learns hospitality.
Arab

501. Only the innkeeper is unworried by his guests' big appetites. *Chinese*

502. To issue an invitation is to render ourselves responsible for our guest's happiness as long as he is under our roof. *French*

503. The guest is dearest when he is leaving. *German*

504. The other man's bread tastes sweeter. *Greek*

505. A person is a guest for one or two days, but becomes an intruder on the third. *Hindustan*

506. A guest between two houses will starve. *India*

507. Do not visit too often or too long. *Irish*

508. While there's fire in one's cooking stove, guests will never cease to arrive. *Japanese*

509. An uninvited guest is worse than a Tartar. *Russian*

510. Whether a child, or an old man, or a youth come to thy house, he is to be treated with respect, for of all men thy guest is thy superior. *Sanskrit*

511. Come uncalled, sit unserved. *Scottish*

512. A guest who breaks the dishes of his host is not soon forgotten.   *West Africa*
513. The place of an uninvited guest is behind the door.   *Yugoslav*

Habit

514. I dreamed a thousand new paths...I woke and walked my old one. *Chinese*
515. Filth is got rid of by washing; habit is not so easy to erase. *Hindustan*
516. Old habits are iron shirts. *Yugoslav*

Health

517. No man is a good physician who has never been sick. *Arab*
518. When you shut out the sun from the window, the doctor comes in at the door. *Chinese*
519. An apple a day keeps the doctor away. *English*
520. The purse of the patient protracts his cure. *German*

521. Death is the doctor of all incurable ills. *Greek*
522. A disease comes with the speed of an elephant, and goes with the speed of an ant. *India*
523. A good laugh and a long sleep are the best cures in the doctor's book. *Irish*
524. Sickness is the physician's feast. *Irish*
525. The herb that can't be got is the one that brings relief. *Irish*
526. The more you think of dying, the better you will live. *Italian*
527. He who is afflicted can best appreciate health. *Persian*
528. See the pale color of my face and do not ask after my health. *Persian*
529. Expensive remedies are always useful, if not to the sick, to the chemist. *Russian*
530. A patient will never recover his health merely from the description of a medicine. *Sanskrit*
531. None are so well as they that hope to be better. *Scottish*
532. When he sees death, then he is willing to accept fever. *Turkish*
533. Good thoughts are half of health. *Yugoslav*

HINDSIGHT

534. When the ship has sunk, everyone knows how she could have been saved. *Italian*
535. Now that I put my hand to my head, I see there is no hat. *Persian*

HUNGER

536. Grinding one's teeth does not fill one's belly. *Arab*
537. She was so hungry she couldn't stay for the parson to say grace. *English*
538. The way to a man's heart is through his stomach. *English*
539. Hunger is the best cook. *German*
540. Hunger is content with any food and sleep with any bed. *Hindustan*
541. Of what use is a blush on the face if the stomach is empty? *India*
542. No one ever washes himself so as never to require it again, nor does anyone ever eat so as to never hunger again. *India*
543. God never sent hunger without something to satisfy it. *Irish*

544. Happiness rarely keeps company with an empty stomach. *Japanese*

545. Hunger is a good kitchen to a cold potato. *Scottish*

546. There is no sauce like a good appetite. *Spanish*

547. A hungry monkey will not dance. *Turkish*

548. What do the satiated know of how the hungry feel? *Turkish*

549. No bread is too sharp to be refused by hunger. *Yugoslav*

7

IMPOSSIBILITIES

550. Though the emperor be rich, he cannot buy one extra year.   *Chinese*

551. You can't make a silk purse out of a sow's ear. *English*

552. It's a bad bridge that is shorter than its stream. *German*

553. You cannot hide behind your finger.   *Greek*

554. How can a sleeping man wake another who is asleep?   *Hindustan*

555. Money seen in a dream will not be available for one's expenses.   *India*

556. You cannot get milk from a male buffalo, nor butter by churning water.   *India*

557. Water will not divide if you strike it with a stick. *India*

558. You can't take more out of a bag than what's in it. *Irish*

559. A knife will not cut its own handle. *Persian*

560. You cannot have the skin twice from the same bull. *Russian*

561. You can't drive straight on a twisting lane. *Russian*

562. The tip of a finger cannot be touched by itself. *Sanskrit*

563. You can't ring the bell and at the same time walk in the procession. *Spanish*

564. A mouth does not get sweet by talking about honey. *Turkish*

565. Even the best cooking pot will not produce food. *West Africa*

INDUSTRY AND SLOTH

566. Ask God for as much as you like, but keep a spade in your hand. *Armenian*

567. Better return home and make a net than go down to the river and desire to get fishes. *Chinese*

568. Work with the rising sun, rest with the setting sun.   *Chinese*
569. The devil finds work for idle hands.   *English*
570. Rolling stones gather no moss.   *English*
571. To make an omelet, you have to break an egg.   *French*
572. God gives the nuts, but he does not crack them.   *German*
573. Not the butterfly but the bee produces the honey.   *Greek*
574. He who is too lazy to crack the nuts will have none to eat.   *Greek*
575. Come, friend, and be doing something. It is better to work for nothing than to be idle.   *Hindustan*
576. The man who works like a slave may eat like a king.   *India*
577. A sleeping cat cannot catch a rat.   *India*
578. There is no need to fear the wind if your haystacks are tied down.   *Irish*
579. 'Tis the quiet people that do the work.   *Italian*
580. In the house where the samisen is played all day long, there will be little rice in the larder.   *Japanese*

581. "If" was married to "But" and they had a child named "Would-it-be." *Persian*

582. Better to beg than steal, but better to work than beg. *Russian*

583. No sweat, no sweet. *Scottish*

584. The fields are ever frozen for lazy pigs. *Swedish*

585. He who would climb a palm tree must not rest at its foot. *West Africa*

586. Who wishes to rest when he gets old ought to work while he is young. *Yugoslav*

INGRATITUDE

587. He gets his passage for nothing and then winks at the captain's wife. *Arab*

588. Warm up a frozen snake and she will bite you. *Armenian*

589. In the theater, free seats hiss first. *Chinese*

590. Don't look a gift horse in the mouth. *English*

591. Who serves his country often serves an ingrate. *French*

592. Swift gratitude is the sweetest. *Greek*

593. I gave him a staff for his support and he uses it to break my head. *India*

594. The temple has fallen on the head of him that went to worship.   *India*

595. If you beg on a foolscap, don't thank on a postcard. *Irish*

596. A satiated mouth soon forgets the benefactor. *Japanese*

597. Give the naked a piece of cloth and he will say it is too thick.   *Russian*

598. Give a beggar a bed and he'll repay you with a louse.   *Scottish*

599. He who has drunk his fill soon turns his back on the fountain.   *Spanish*

600. Scarcely has the hungry beggar-woman eaten her fill than she wants us to call her Madam. *Yugoslav*

𝒥

❦

JUDGMENT

601. Don't judge a book by its cover.   *English*
602. He measures others by himself.   *French*
603. Do not judge until you have heard both sides of the argument.   *Greek*
604. When a camel is at the foot of a mountain, then judge his height.   *Hindustan*
605. He who would form a correct judgment of their tone must hear first one bell and then the other.   *Italian*
606. The fiddle is judged by its tune.   *Russian*

JUSTICE AND INJUSTICE

607. Though the sword of justice be sharp, it will not slay the innocent. *Chinese*

608. Justice is ever on the side of the victor. *French*

609. The poor man must suffer for the rich man's transgressions. *German*

610. The edge cuts and the sword has the credit; the soldiers fight and the general has the fame. *Hindustan*

611. If a man steals gold, he is put in prison. If he steals a land, he is made king. *Japanese*

612. To spare the ravening leopard is an act of injustice to the sheep. *Persian*

613. The bear does the dancing and the gypsy takes the money. *Russian*

614. The way of justice is mysterious. *Sanskrit*

615. They first hang a man, then try him. *Scottish*

616. The rich break the laws and the poor are punished for it. *Spanish*

617. The dog stole and the goat is being punished. *West Africa*

618. Injustice laughs by the table while justice weeps behind the door. *Yugoslav*

LAWS

619. Win your lawsuit and lose your money. *Chinese*

620. It's an ill cause a lawyer thinks shame of. *English*

621. Men make laws, but women make morals. *French*

622. Go to law for a sheep and you lose your cow.
German

623. As fast as laws are devised, their evasion is
contrived. *German*

624. Lawsuits make the parties lean, the lawyers fat.
German

625. When a law is made, the way to avoid it is
discovered. *Italian*

626. A nobleman is always in the right when a peasant
sues. *Russian*

627. The law is like the axle of a carriage; you can turn it wherever you please.   *Russian*
628. A good lawyer may be an ill neighbor.   *Scottish*
629. Laws, like the spider's web, catch the fly and let the hawk go free.   *Spanish*
630. When a bribe enters the door, laws get out at the chimney.   *Turkish*
631. Where there is no law, there can be no infraction of the same.   *Yugoslav*

LOVE

632. Love is blind.   *English*
633. Love is not to be trifled with.   *French*
634. Who loves well, forgets slowly.   *French*
635. He who hates is to be pitied, but he who loves is to be pitied more.   *German*
636. Love can turn the cottage into a golden palace. *German*
637. The heart that loves is always young.   *Greek*
638. The ways of love are peculiar to itself.   *Hindustan*
639. When the heart clings to a lover, who cares what caste he be?   *India*
640. If you live in my heart, you live rent-free.   *Irish*

641. He who has love in his breast has ever the spurs at his flanks. *Italian*

642. Love feedeth only upon love. *Italian*

643. He who is lucky in love should never play cards. *Italian*

644. She will love tomorrow who loved not yesterday. *Italian*

645. Who travels for love, finds a thousand miles only one mile. *Japanese*

646. Love does not recognize a difference between peasant and mikado. *Japanese*

647. A lass that has many wooers often chooses the worst. *Scottish*

648. Love kills with golden arrows. *Spanish*

649. It is never too far to the home of your beloved. *Swedish*

650. Before you love, learn to run through snow leaving no footprints. *Turkish*

651. A lovesick person looks in vain for a doctor. *West Africa*

MARRIAGE

652. The joys of life are porridge and soup, a donkey to ride and a wife to drive it. *Arab*

653. Who marries for love without money has good nights and sorry days. *English*

654. Marriage teaches you to live alone. *French*

655. A priest will perform your marriage ceremony, but he will not manage your house. *India*

656. Let the man that you marry have an old maid for a mother. *Irish*

657. If the hen crows instead of the cock, there won't be peace in the fowlyard. *Japanese*

658. A man without a wife is like a man in winter without a fur cap. *Russian*

659. Woe is the wife who lacks a tongue, but well's the man who gets her. *Scottish*

660. Never marry a widow unless her first husband was hanged. *Scottish*

661. He who tells his wife all is but newly married. *Scottish*

662. If your wife tells you to throw yourself off a cliff, pray to God that it is a low one. *Spanish*

663. A good wife is the workmanship of a good husband. *Spanish*

664. If you look for a faultless woman, you will remain a bachelor. *Turkish*

665. Buy all the presents you will, if a woman does not love you, she is bound to marry another. *West Africa*

666. Differences between husband and wife should not be aired in the marketplace. *West Africa*

667. Where there is no wife, there is no home. *Yugoslav*

MISFORTUNE AND FORTUNE

668. After sorrow comes joy. *Arab*

669. Throw him into the river and he will rise with a fish in his mouth. *Arab*

670. If I were to trade in winding sheets, no one would die. *Arab*

671. Blessings never come in pairs and ills never come alone. *Chinese*

672. It never rains, but it pours. *English*

673. If he flings a penny in the air, a dollar will come down to him. *English*

674. We must learn from life how to suffer it. *French*

675. He who has not tasted bitter, knows not what sweet is. *German*

676. One gets pears without asking, and another cannot obtain alms even by begging. *Hindustan*

677. A coming misfortune must be borne with patience; when it is gone you are liberated. *Hindustan*

678. All are ready to be partners in a man's successes, none in his misfortunes. *India*

679. When the elephant sinks in a pit, even the frog gives him a backward kick. *India*

680. If I bet on the tide, it wouldn't come in. *Irish*

681. He who would have no trouble in this world must not be born in it. *Italian*

682. A sorrow is an itching place that is made worse by scratching. *Japanese*

683. The heaviest rains fall on the leakiest house. *Japanese*

684. Advise and counsel him. If he does not listen, let adversity teach him. *Japanese*

685. Walk fast and you catch misfortune; walk slowly and it catches you. *Russian*

686. Fortune and misfortune dwell in the same courtyard. *Russian*

687. Good fortune wears a pretty dress but its underclothes do not bear investigation. *Russian*

688. Running away through fear of a scorpion, he falls into the jaws of a poisonous snake. *Sanskrit*

689. He that has his hand in the lion's mouth must take it out the best way he can. *Scottish*

690. Trouble will rain on those who are already wet. *Spanish*

691. Compare your griefs with other men's and they will seem less. *Spanish*

692. It won't get better until worse has passed. *Swedish*

693. He ran away from the rain and was caught in a hailstorm. *Turkish*

694. If you have escaped the jaws of the crocodile while bathing in the river, you will surely meet a leopard on the way.   *West Africa*

695. If Fortune does not wait for you, you cannot overtake her even with the fastest steed.   *Yugoslav*

MONEY

696. He that has no money has no friends.   *Arab*

697. A girl with a golden cradle doesn't remain long in her father's house.   *Armenian*

698. A poor man associating with a rich man will soon be too poor to buy even a pair of breeches.
Chinese

699. He has a hole under his nose that all of his money runs into.   *English*

700. A penny saved is a penny earned.   *English*

701. A fool and his money are soon parted.   *English*

702. A purse without money is but a piece of leather.   *English*

703. All that glitters is not gold.   *English*

704. A covetous man makes a halfpenny of a farthing, and a liberal man makes sixpence of it.   *English*

705. He who has money receives more.   *French*

706. Good bargains empty our pockets. *German*
707. Five drachmas in the hand is better than ten drachmas on paper. *Greek*
708. When you know you are about to lose all your wealth, then you had better give half of it away. *Hindustan*
709. The offense given by not lending is to be preferred to the annoyance endured after lending. *India*
710. A heavy purse makes a light heart. *Irish*
711. Does your neighbor bore you? Lend him some money. *Italian*
712. Who would make money must begin by spending it. *Italian*
713. He who pays well is master of everybody's purse. *Italian*
714. If a few sen do not go, many sen will not come. *Japanese*
715. Do not look at the gold pieces you won; rather consider those you might have lost. *Japanese*
716. Credit is better than wealth. *Persian*
717. Where gold speaketh, all is silent. *Russian*
718. A penniless man goes fast through the market. *Scottish*

719. He who would be rich has not to pick up money, but to diminish his wants.   *Spanish*
720. Love of money is the undoing of men.   *West Africa*
721. A castle offered for a dinar is dear when you have no dinar.   *Yugoslav*

𝒫

PATIENCE

722. The remedy against bad times is to be patient with them.   *Arab*

723. Patience and a mulberry leaf will make a silk gown.   *Chinese*

724. Everything comes to him who waits.   *English*

725. Patience is bitter, but its fruit is sweet.   *French*

726. Patience is often better than medicine.   *German*

727. Patience caught the nimble hare.   *Greek*

728. Patience cures many an old complaint.   *Irish*

729. He that hath no patience, hath nothing at all.   *Italian*

730. The string of a man's sack of patience is generally tied with a slip knot.   *Japanese*

731. The future belongs to him who knows how to wait.   *Russian*

732. There is summer and there is winter; what need for hurry?   *Turkish*

733. Patience can break through iron doors.   *Yugoslav*

PERSISTENCE

734. If you cannot take things by the head, then take them by the tail.   *Arab*

735. Great things can be reduced to small things, and small things can be reduced to nothing.   *Chinese*

736. Little strokes fell great oaks.   *English*

737. Practice makes perfect.   *English*

738. If at first you don't succeed, try, try, again. *English*

739. A road of a thousand miles begins with the first step.   *English*

740. There is no mortar that time shall not loosen. *French*

741. He that would climb the ladder must begin at the bottom.   *German*

742. If you seek well, you will find.   *Greek*

743. He who has lost his way in the morning cannot be said to have gone astray if he finds the way at night. *Hindustan*

744. If you throw a handful of stones, one at least will hit. *India*

745. Fall seven times, stand up the eighth time. *Japanese*

746. An apprentice becomes an expert by and by. *Persian*

747. Hair by hair, you may pluck out the whole beard. *Russian*

748. If you would be Pope, you can think of nothing else. *Spanish*

749. When a shepherd has a mind to do so, he will get you milk from a he-goat. *Turkish*

750. The monkey learns to jump by trying again and again. *West Africa*

POVERTY

751. Riches disclose bad qualities which poverty conceals. *Arab*

752. The rich man plans for tomorrow, the poor man for today. *Chinese*

753. Better die ten years early than live ten years poor.
Chinese

754. From poverty to profusion is a hard journey, but the way back is easy. *Japanese*

755. Troubles rain from walls and doors for a poor man. *Persian*

756. Poverty is the heritage of poverty. *Russian*

757. If everyone gives a kopeck, the poor will have a ruble. *Russian*

758. The defect of poverty is the destroyer of a host of virtues. *Sanskrit*

759. Poverty is a pain but not a disgrace. *Scottish*

760. When your own possessions are gone, those of another are of little use. *West Africa*

PREFERABLE ALTERNATIVES

761. Better a diamond with a flaw than a pebble without one. *English*

762. Half a loaf is better than none. *English*

763. Better late than never. *English*

764. To be redheaded is better than to be without a head. *Irish*

765. Better wisdom than riches. *Swedish*

766. Better coarse bread than none to eat.   *Swedish*

PREMATURITY

767. Do not count the days of a month which may never belong to you.   *Arab*

768. With one hand he feeds the hens, with the other he searches for eggs.   *Armenian*

769. Don't count your chickens before they're hatched.   *English*

770. Chickens are slow in coming from unlaid eggs.   *German*

771. Never promise a fish until it's caught.   *Irish*

772. Do not sell the skin before catching the gazelle.   *Persian*

773. He who anticipates good fortune risks it by his presumption.   *Spanish*

774. Don't turn up your trousers before you get to the brook.   *Turkish*

775. Don't go selling the hide as long as the bear remains in his hole.   *Yugoslav*

PRIDE

776. He that is proud of his fine clothes gets his reputation from his tailor. *English*
777. When a proud man hears another praised, he thinks himself injured. *English*
778. It is easier to lift the mountain on the point of a needle than to root out pride from the heart. *German*
779. The barber washes everyone's feet, but thinks it beneath him to wash his own. *Hindustan*
780. The house of pride is usually empty. *India*
781. Pride is the authority of every sin. *Irish*
782. Brag not of the honor of ancestors. All you have is your own. *Swedish*

QUARRELS

783. Wrath begins in madness and ends in repentance.
   Arab

784. Whilst wrangling over a quarter of pig, you lose a flock of sheep.   *Chinese*

785. A man that will fight may find a cudgel in every hedge.   *English*

786. Quarrels would not last long if the wrongs were all on one side.   *French*

787. Not to be on speaking terms is better than quarreling.   *India*

788. A minute's parlaying is better than a week's fighting.   *Irish*

789. Who seeks a quarrel will find it near at hand.
Italian

790. The second word makes the fray. *Japanese*

791. If two men quarrel, even their dogs will have a difference. *Japanese*

792. A bad peace is better than a good quarrel. *Russian*

793. It's an ill fight where he that wins has the worst of it. *Scottish*

794. It is seldom the fault of one when two argue. *Swedish*

795. If you say "all right," there will be no quarrel in the bath. *Turkish*

796. Every tree has a thick end, and every quarrel has a cause. *West Africa*

797. Better a spoon of juice in peace than a table laden with food in a quarrel. *Yugoslav*

RATIONALIZATION

798. Because the cat was given no meat, he said it was Friday. *Armenian*

799. To the bad driver, the mules are always to blame. *Greek*

800. He that cannot dance claims the floor is uneven. *Hindustan*

801. He fell down and said he was bowing to a god; he got swollen and claimed he was getting fat. *India*

802. The fox has no desire for cherries because he has not learned how to climb the tree. *Italian*

803. He is alive for he cannot afford a funeral. *Persian*

804. "Why fuss about it?" said the crane after the eel had slipped away. "I never liked fish anyway."
West Africa

REALITY

805. It is only when the cold season comes that we know the pine and cypress to be evergreens.   *Chinese*

806. If you walk on snow you cannot hide your footprints.   *Chinese*

807. There is no rose without a thorn.   *English*

808. Beard and mantle do not make one a philosopher.
German

809. He keeps Lent because he has nothing to eat.
Greek

810. No proof is required of what is before our eyes.
Hindustan

811. The humpback alone knows how he can lie comfortably.   *India*

812. He who bears the burden on his shoulders knows its weight.   *India*

813. Those who travel on horseback know nothing of the toil of those who travel on foot.   *Japanese*

814. The ass is the same ass even when his halter has been changed. *Persian*

815. He who sows barley cannot gather wheat. *Persian*

816. By slitting the ears and cutting the tail, a dog is still a dog, not a horse, not an ass. *Sanskrit*

817. A dog does not resent being called a dog. *West Africa*

818. The child of a leopard is a leopard. *West Africa*

RELATIVITY

819. Where there are no green trees, the castor oil bush is regarded as one. *India*

820. To the ant, a few drops of rain is a flood. *Japanese*

821. Where the camel is sold for a cent, the ass has no actual value. *Persian*

822. He who has never seen a castle will admire a pigpen. *Yugoslav*

RELIGION

823. You honor dead Buddhas, but the living Buddhas you do not honor. *Chinese*

824. They that are in hell think there is no heaven. *English*

825. God helps those who help themselves.   *English*

826. If the triangles made a god, they would give him three sides.   *French*

827. The devil laughs if a thief steals from another thief.   *French*

828. The universe is a thought from God.   *German*

829. A pack of cards is the devil's prayerbook.   *German*

830. The fewer the words, the better the prayer.   *German*

831. Why burn oil before the ikon while you swear at God?   *Greek*

832. The devil invented war and fools practice it.   *Greek*

833. Light your lamp first at home and only afterwards at the mosque.   *Hindustan*

834. God never closed one gap without opening another.   *Irish*

835. You worship God in your way and I'll worship Him in His.   *Irish*

836. He who leaves God out of his reckoning does not know how to count.   *Italian*

837. Begin your web and God will supply the thread.   *Italian*

838. One word of thanks reaches up to heaven.
Japanese

839. Go before God with justice, before the judge with money. *Russian*

840. Where God builds his church, there the devil has his chapel. *Russian*

841. Give the devil a candle as well; you never know whom you may please. *Russian*

842. Even the thief prays to God, but the devil gets hold of his prayers. *Russian*

843. God is always where we don't look for him. *Russian*

844. Pray to God, but do not offend the devil either. *Russian*

845. Pray to God but keep rowing to the shore. *Russian*

846. Non-injury is the highest religion. *Sanskrit*

847. The closer to the church one lives, the more often he is late for mass. *Yugoslav*

848. God shuts one door in order to open a hundred doors. *Yugoslav*

RESIGNATION

849. He who has put his head into the mortar should not be afraid of the bellows.   *Hindustan*

850. Since my house must be burned, I may as well warm myself at it.   *Italian*

851. When the water is overhead, what difference if it be one fathom or a hundred fathoms?   *Persian*

SECRECY

852. Do not tell secrets in front of servants. *Arab*

853. A man's folly ought to be his greatest secret.
English

854. Every betrayal of a secret is the fault of the person
who confided it. *French*

855. Secret charity and secret patience are best. *German*

856. The drunkard and the fool never keep secrets.
Greek

857. If only one knows it, it is secret; if two know it, it
is public. *India*

858. He who comes to you with a secret to tell goes
away with two. *Irish*

859. He who wishes another to guard his secret should guard it himself first. *Italian*

860. The bosoms of the wise are the tombs of secrets. *Japanese*

861. Talk quietly; even the walls have ears. *Persian*

862. When the scabbards are broken, we can no longer hide our swords. *Russian*

863. Keep no secrets from your doctor, your confessor, and your lawyer. *Spanish*

864. A discreet man will always be ignorant of more than he knows. *Spanish*

SEQUENCES

865. When the fingers fall to scratching, the thumb follows along. *Chinese*

866. Where the needle goes, the thread follows. *India*

867. Where the head goes, the feet will go also. *Turkish*

868. I am scratching myself where I am itching. *Yugoslav*

SPEECH

869. More than one war has been caused by a single word. *Arab*

870. If you wish to know the mind of a man, listen to his speech. *Chinese*

871. To lock up mischief, keep your mouth closed. *Chinese*

872. Fair words make me look to my purse. *English*

873. The tongue of a fool carves a piece of his heart to all that sit near him. *English*

874. What orators lack in depth, they make up for in length. *French*

875. The spoken word belongs half to him who speaks and half to him who hears. *French*

876. The wise man weighs his words on the goldsmith's scale. *German*

877. Words often do worse than blows. *German*

878. A man has two ears and one mouth that he hear much and speak little. *German*

879. Not speech, but facts, convince. *Greek*

880. The sword in its scabbard, and the tongue in its place, will never cause tears to be shed. *Greek*

881. No sooner have you spoken than what you have said becomes the property of another. *Hindustan*

882. That which is in the mind comes into the mouth. *Hindustan*

883. Where there is a surfeit of words, there is a famine of intelligence. *India*

884. One lash to a good horse, one word to a sensible man. *India*

885. Soft words butter not turnips, but they won't harden the heart of the cabbage either. *Irish*

886. A sweet tongue is seldom without a sting to its root. *Irish*

887. God gave us two ears and one mouth and we should use them in the same proportion. *Irish*

888. Don't let your tongue say what your head may pay for. *Italian*

889. Many have suffered for talking; none ever suffered for keeping silent. *Italian*

890. What shall I say when it is better to say nothing? *Italian*

891. To quarrel with a man of good speech is better than to converse with a man of rude address. *Sanskrit*

892. Talking is easy, action is difficult. *Spanish*

893. A pleasant tongue will lure a snake out of its hole. *Turkish*

894. Why keep on talking when we know you so well? *West Africa*

SUPERFLUITY

895. On a rainy day many offer to water the chickens.
Armenian

896. He that is baldheaded has no need of combs.   *India*

897. When one has no needle, thread is of little use.
Japanese

898. No fishes are required in a pond which has no
water.   *Persian*

899. To make a present to the rich is to throw water into
the sea.   *Russian*

900. A blacksmith has no need of an axe.   *West Africa*

SUPERIORITY

901. He whose virtues exceed his talents is a superior
man; he whose talents exceed his virtues is an
inferior man.   *Chinese*

902. Men carry their superiority inside, animals
outside.   *Russian*

SUSPICION

903. If you would avoid suspicion, don't lace your shoes
in a melon field.   *Chinese*

904. Shake a bridle over a Yorkshireman's grave and he'll rise and steal the horse.   *English*

905. When the fox preaches, look to your geese.   *German*

906. Where you hear there are plenty of cherries, always carry a small basket.   *Greek*

907. You make a pretense of preserving the hair while you are cutting off the head.   *India*

908. Never shave a corpse alone, for fear your hand would slip and you'd be accused of murder.   *Irish*

909. I know they are all honest men, but my cloak is nowhere to be found.   *Spanish*

Teachers

910. A good teacher is better than a barrelful of books. *Chinese*
911. Whoever cares to learn will always find a teacher. *German*
912. With whatever teachers you mingle, such letters you will learn. *Greek*
913. Drink water after straining, and adopt a teacher after you know him. *Hindustan*
914. As is the teacher, so will the scholar be. *India*
915. If the teacher be corrupt, the world will be corrupt. *Persian*

THRIFT AND PRUDENCE

916. A stitch in time saves nine.   *English*

917. Ask your purse what you should buy.   *English*

918. A blanket is not to be thrown away because of lice.   *Hindustan*

919. Don't throw away your dirty water until you have got clean.   *Irish*

920. A man who always wears his best kimono has no Sunday clothes.   *Japanese*

921. If you have eaten the morsel on Wednesday, do not look for it on Thursday.   *Russian*

922. Buy what you don't need and you'll sell what you can't spare.   *Scottish*

923. The one who saves something has something.   *Swedish*

924. When the soup is boiling over, a ladle is not too costly.   *Turkish*

925. If you would eat eggs, take care of the hen.   *West Africa*

926. He who does not mend old clothes will not wear new ones.   *Yugoslav*

927. He who works has much; he who saves, still more.   *Yugoslav*

928. If a man does not begin saving while the sack of wheat is full, he will not save when the wheat is at the bottom of the sack.   *Yugoslav*

TIMELINESS

929. Make your bargains before beginning to plow.   *Arab*

930. After they had ravished her, she called out to the night watchman.   *Arab*

931. Clean the drainpipes while it is still good weather.   *Chinese*

932. Water which is distant is no good for a fire which is near.   *Chinese*

933. Make hay while the sun shines.   *English*

934. Strike while the iron is hot.   *English*

935. The early bird gets the worm.   *English*

936. Never put off until tomorrow what you can do today.   *English*

937. 'Tis not enough to run well, unless you set out in due time.   *French*

938. He that always thinks it is too soon is sure to come too late.   *German*

939. The wolf that measures the distance goes hungry. *Greek*

940. Today is, tomorrow is not.   *Hindustan*

941. Everything must wait its turn...peach blossoms for the second month and chrysanthemums for the ninth.   *Japanese*

942. When you're thirsty, it's too late to think about digging a well.   *Japanese*

943. An incident should be remedied before it occurs. *Persian*

944. By the time you put on your arms, the war is finished.   *Persian*

945. It is too late to think of wine when the cask is empty.   *Russian*

946. Time does not bow to you, you must bow to time. *Russian*

947. After the daughter is married, then we find many would-be-sons-in-law.   *Russian*

948. A thing done at a wrong time should be regarded as not done.   *Sanskrit*

949. The road of by and by leads to the house of never.   *Spanish*

950. What is not done on its day will not be done in a year. *Turkish*

TRAVEL

951. He that has long legs travels far. *Arab*

952. The mile is long to him who is tired. *Japanese*

953. On a long journey, even a straw weighs heavy. *Spanish*

954. Who makes frequent inquiries about the road does not go astray. *Yugoslav*

TRUTH AND FALSEHOOD

955. Always tell the truth in the form of a joke. *Armenian*

956. One man tells a lie, dozens repeat it as the truth. *Chinese*

957. Honesty is the best policy. *English*

958. Only truth is beautiful. *French*

959. A liar isn't believed even when he tells the truth. *German*

960. Truth ill-timed is as bad as a lie. *German*

961. Truth gives a short answer; lies go roundabout. *German*

962. A lie becomes true when one believes it.   *German*
963. Truths are not uttered from behind masks.   *Greek*
964. A tongue's slip is a truth's revelation.   *Greek*
965. Rogues listen not to discourses on honesty.   *India*
966. There are more lies told at a wake than in a courtroom.   *Irish*
967. A little truth helps the lie go down.   *Italian*
968. Oil and truth will get uppermost last.   *Italian*
969. A lie has no legs but scandalous wings.   *Japanese*
970. The wise man says "I am looking for truth," and the fool, "I have found truth."   *Russian*
971. Bury truth in a golden coffin and it will break it open.   *Russian*
972. The dexterous make even untruths appear truths as those skilled in painting can make hollows and eminences on a level surface.   *Sanskrit*
973. Do not lie for want of news.   *Scottish*
974. To listen to a lie is harder than to tell it.   *Turkish*
975. The liar's house was burning but no one would believe it.   *Turkish*
976. Tell a lie on Saturday and you will be ashamed on Sunday.   *Turkish*

977. Truth keeps the hand cleaner than soap.
West Africa

978. A lie has seven variation, the truth none.
West Africa

979. Speak the truth, but leave immediately after.
Yugoslav

980. A lie has short legs.   *Yugoslav*

U

USELESS PURSUITS

981. The cat, though blind, still hankers after mice.
Arab

982. Music helps not the toothache. *English*

983. When a man is dead there is no use calling the doctor. *French*

984. It is little use to dig a well after the house has caught on fire. *Hindustan*

985. It's no use carrying an umbrella if your shoes are leaking. *Irish*

986. One cannot learn to swim in a field. *Japanese*

987. No applause can be made with one hand. *Persian*

988. Throwing pebbles at an elephant in no way disturbs him. *West Africa*

VALUE

989. A man's value is that which he sets upon himself.   *French*

990. The scales tell us what is light and what is heavy, but not what is gold and what is silver.   *German*

991. Pearls are of no value in a desert.   *Hindustan*

992. One does not know the worth of teeth while they last.   *India*

993. An empty house gives better value to its owner than an owing tenant.   *Irish*

VANITY

994. The rooster that crows too long tires his own throat.   *Greek*

995. I'd make money if I could buy him for any price and sell him at his own.   *Irish*

996. Don't remind a vain man of his pimples.   *Russian*

997. Self-praise smells bad.   *Swedish*

WISDOM

998. The eyes are of little use if the mind be blind.
Arab

999. See that you are wise, but also learn how to appear ignorant. *Armenian*

1000. A man cannot leave his wisdom or his experience to his heirs. *Italian*

1001. Wisdom is born; stupidity is learned. *Russian*